WORLD HOLIDAYS

Therese Harasymiw

REAL LIFE readers™

Rosen Classroom™

New York

Published in 2009 by The Rosen Publishing Group, Inc.
29 East 21st Street, New York, NY 10010

Book Design: Michael J. Flynn

Photo Credits: Cover © John Leung/Shutterstock; p. 5 (family celebrating Kwanzaa) © Yellow Dog Productions/The Image Bank/Getty Images; p. 5 (box of chocolates) © Hallgerd/Shutterstock; p. 5 (bagpipe players) © Pres Panayotov/Shutterstock; p. 6 © Jorge Silva/AFP/Getty Images; p. 9 (Queen Victoria) © Hulton Archive/Getty Images; p. 9 (fireworks) © Elena Elisseeva/Shutterstock; p. 11 © James L. Stanfield/National Geographic/Getty Images; p. 12 © Koksharov Dmitry/Shutterstock; p. 13 © Sean Garnsworthy/Getty Images; p. 14 © Toshifumi/AFP/Getty Images; p. 17 © Jorge Uzon/AFP/Getty Images; p. 18 © Alex Wong/Getty Images; p. 21 © Kambou/AFP/Getty Images.

ISBN: 978-1-4358-0129-5
6-pack ISBN: 978-1-4358-0130-1

Manufactured in the United States of America

CPSIA Compliance Infomation: Batch #WR212070RC:
For Further Information contact Rosen Publishing, New York, New York at 1-800-237-9932

CONTENTS

HOLIDAYS AROUND THE WORLD

Do you like to give cards on Valentine's Day or make dinner on Thanksgiving? On holidays, we set aside our everyday jobs and tasks. We do special things to remember important people, events, or ideas.

People all over the world have holidays. Some holidays are **celebrated** in several countries. Some are celebrated in just one country. Let's learn about some holidays around the world and the ways people celebrate them.

Do you have a favorite holiday? Do you know what holidays are shown in these pictures?

These people are gathered in Mexico City to watch fireworks marking Mexico's Independence Day.

INDEPENDENCE DAYS

Each year on July 4, people in the United States celebrate Independence Day. "Independence" means "freedom." Americans remember how the United States formed a new nation after becoming free from British rule. People enjoy parades, cookouts, games, and music. In some places, colorful fireworks are part of the celebration.

Other countries have independence days when they celebrate becoming free and independent nations. Mexico celebrates independence from Spain on September 16, and India celebrates its independence from Britain on August 15.

VICTORIA DAY

Queen Victoria was the ruler of the British **Empire** from 1837 to 1901. Canada was ruled by Britain from 1763 until it gained full independence in 1931. Canada still honors Britain and Queen Victoria's birthday with a holiday. Victoria Day is **observed** on the Monday before May 25 each year.

Like other holidays, Victoria Day is celebrated with parades and music. Often, the British flag is flown next to Canada's flag. This reminds Canadians of the bond between Canada and Britain.

Toronto, Canada, celebrates its British ties on Victoria Day with fireworks displays.

Queen Victoria

BASTILLE DAY

Bastille (baa-STEEL) Day is a French holiday celebrated on July 14. It's named for a prison that was once in Paris, France. In the late 1700s, many French people were unhappy with their king. They wanted a new government and more control over making laws. On July 14, 1789, a large group of people attacked the Bastille to show their power.

Today, Bastille Day is a time to remember how the French people shaped their government. There are parades around the place where the Bastille once stood and even dancing in the streets!

This painting shows an artist's idea of the attack on the Bastille in 1789.

CAUSE

French people wanted a new government.

EFFECT

They took over the Bastille to show their power and later formed a new government.

BOXING DAY

On December 26, people in Britain, Australia, New Zealand, and Canada celebrate Boxing Day. It's called "boxing" day because people fill boxes with gifts. No one knows when or how this holiday started. It may come from the **Middle Ages**, when wealthy people gave their workers gifts on December 26. Later, it became a day to give money and gifts to the poor and to people who have service jobs, such as mail carriers.

Today, Boxing Day is a day to spend time with family and friends. Many people use this day to shop and watch sports as well.

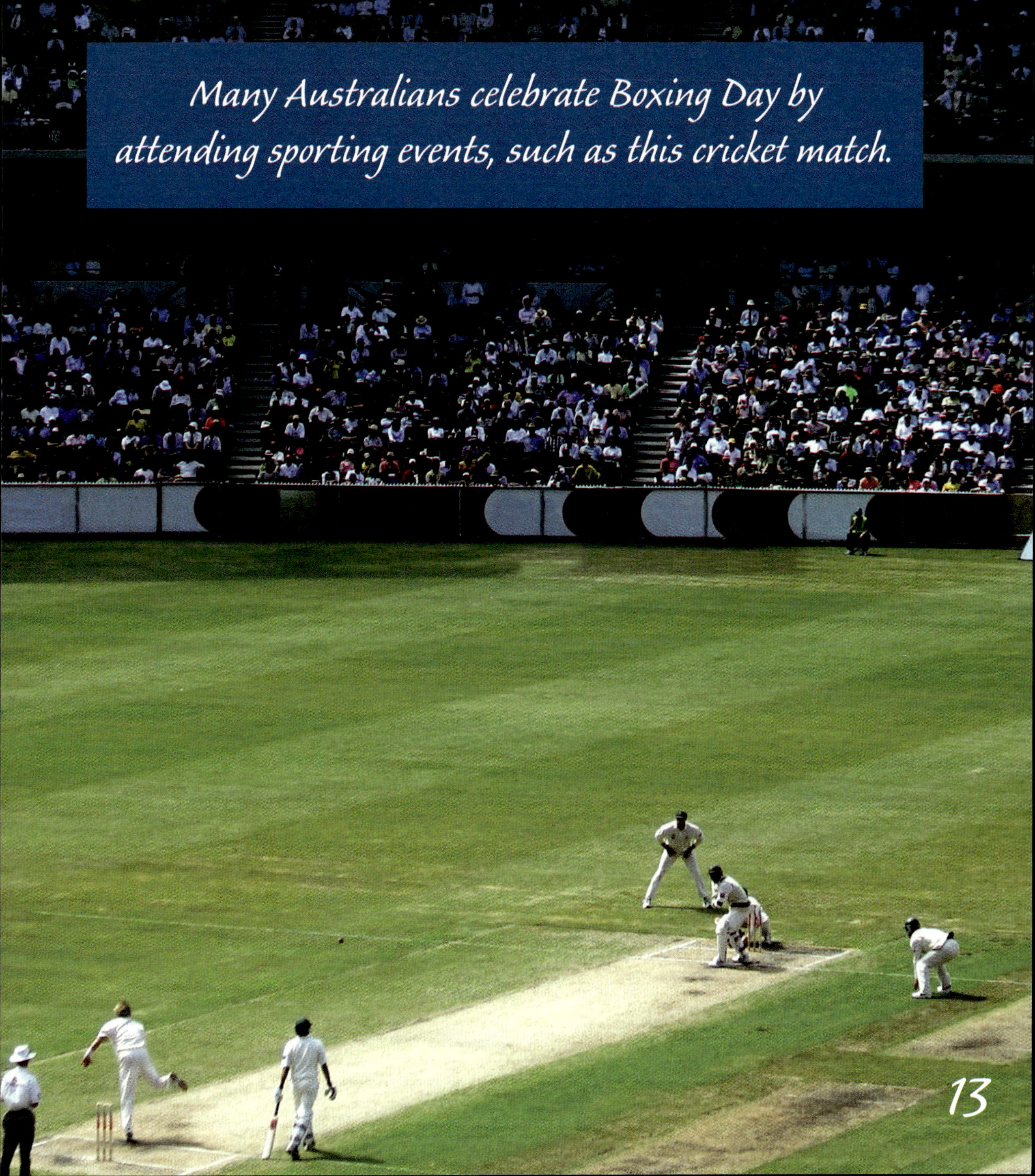

Many Australians celebrate Boxing Day by attending sporting events, such as this cricket match.

These children are marching in a parade in Tokyo, Japan, on Constitution Memorial Day.

CONSTITUTION MEMORIAL DAY

Many countries have holidays to honor their laws and national **constitutions**. In Japan, Constitution **Memorial** Day takes place on May 3 each year. This is during Golden Week, when people take time off from work to celebrate the government, nature, and children.

On Constitution Memorial Day, the national government building is opened to everyone. People think about what **democracy** means to Japan. They study Japanese laws and their effects. They talk about what laws should change and what laws should remain.

CINCO DE MAYO

Mexicans and Mexican Americans celebrate the holiday Cinco de Mayo (SIHN-koh duh MY-oh). "Cinco de Mayo" is Spanish for "fifth of May."

In the 1860s, France sent an army to take control of Mexico. On May 5, 1862, the Mexican army fought an important battle against the French at Puebla, Mexico. The Mexicans won even though the French army was bigger. Soon after, the Mexicans forced the French to leave their country.

Today, Cinco de Mayo marks the Puebla battle with parades, food, dancing, and music.

These men honor Cinco de Mayo by acting out the 1862 battle between the Mexicans (in red) and the French (in blue).

Dragons represent power in the Chinese culture. They're often featured in Chinese New Year parades.

CHINESE NEW YEAR

Many **cultures** celebrate the New Year. One famous celebration is Chinese New Year, which is also called **Lunar** New Year. Some cultures start the beginning of the year on January 1. However, the Chinese calendar's year begins between January 21 and February 20.

To prepare for Chinese New Year, people clean their homes and buy new clothes. Each family shares a large dinner, usually fish, the night before. At midnight, fireworks often light up the skies. For several days after the new year, people visit their families and friends, decorate with the lucky color red, give gifts of money, and march in parades.

AN AFRICAN HOLIDAY

Africa is made up of many cultures. Several African countries came together in 1958 to discuss matters that were important to all of them. One concern was **foreign** countries ruling Africa. The Africans at the meeting wanted all of Africa to be ruled by Africans. They decided to name April 15 African Freedom Day to honor this idea.

On May 25, 1963, over thirty African countries met again. By this time, two-thirds of the **continent** was independent. They changed the date and the name of the special holiday. African **Liberation** Day is now celebrated each year on May 25.

In this picture, the people of Ghana celebrate their freedom from foreign rule by waving their country's flag.

A Year of World Holidays

Chinese New Year	between January 21 and February 20
Constitution Memorial Day (Japan)	May 3
Cinco De Mayo (Mexico)	May 5
Victoria Day (Canada)	May 25
African Liberation Day	May 25
Independence Day (United States)	July 4
Bastille Day (France)	July 14
Independence Day (India)	August 15
Independence Day (Mexico)	September 16
Boxing Day (Britain, Australia, New Zealand, Canada)	December 26

GLOSSARY

celebrate (SEH-luh-brayt) To honor an important event or idea with special activities.

constitution (kahn-stuh-TOO-shun) The basic rules by which a country or state is governed.

continent (KAHN-tuh-nuhnt) One of Earth's seven large landmasses.

culture (KUHL-chur) The beliefs, practices, and arts of a group of people.

democracy (dih-MAH-kruh-see) A system of government in which people choose leaders and help make laws.

empire (EHM-pyr) Many territories ruled by a single leader.

foreign (FOHR-uhn) Coming from outside one's own country.

liberation (lih-buh-RAY-shun) The act of setting something free.

lunar (LOO-nuhr) Having to do with the moon.

memorial (muh-MOHR-ee-uhl) Something used as a reminder of a person, place, or event.

Middle Ages (MIH-duhl AY-juhz) The period in European history from about A.D. 500 to about 1450.

observe (uhb-ZUHRV) To celebrate.

INDEX

Due to the changing nature of Internet links, The Rosen Publishing Group, Inc., has developed an online list of Web sites related to the subject of this book. This site is updated regularly. Please use this link to access the list: **http://www.rcbmlinks.com/rlr/world**